OVERRATED

A Christian woman's guide to living authentically in a perfection-driven world.

Ashley Schubert

INTRODUCTION

Over-Rated Over-rated. (Clap,clap, clap-clap-clap). Over-rated. (Clap, clap, clap-clap-clap.) I can still hear this chant in my head. I can feel the energy from a packed gym and hear the shoes squeaking on the clean gym floor while basketballs dribbled during warm-ups. This was the chant that we did in high school basketball. It was usually during playoff season when the opposing team was given a high ranking for the wrong reasons. This was usually because that team had an easy schedule and hadn't been tested by playing anyone tough yet. Before we went into a game, we knew who the opposing team had played and who they had beat. We knew their strengths and their weaknesses. We knew their key players to watch out for. And we definitely knew if they were over-rated. Over-rated (clap, clap, clap-clap-clap) the crowd continued to chant as the opponents ran out onto the floor. The goal of this chant was to psych them out and make them believe they were weaker than statistics showed. Weaker than they felt. Weaker than they believed. And honestly, sometimes I think it worked. If the team was thrown off their game, even in the slightest, and started the first quarter in a funk, chances were, we could run the floor and take control of the game. Isn't life like this sometimes? We get into our head that we know things to be true, that we feel a certain way about who we are, who our kids are and what our businesses should do. Only to find out, it's all over-rated. The goal of this book is to show you that all the things the world views as needed, as desired and as normal, most of these

things are just over-rated and not true. If we look at what God's word says is truth; we can determine what is false. When we realize that most of the things we see as necessary: to be a good mom, a good wife, a successful woman or just plain happy, these things don't really matter. We can move past anxiety, past mediocrity and past doubt - and we can move into the life God has planned for us all along.

PREFACE

THE WHY BEHIND THE BOOK:

I knew it was going to be something, I just wasn't sure what or when it would happen. When I first started writing this book, I thought "What is God going to teach me through this?" When I wrote my first book, Raising A Business & Babies, God allowed me to go through some tough trials that included a lot of personal relationship tests and trials. I always tell friends "It's like when I said a big YES to writing a book, God said 'HERE YOU GO'! And he gave me plenty to write about." This time around, it has been no different. The big trial during this writing period has been discovering that my third child has sensory integration issues or as it's sometimes referred to, sensory processing. This new diagnosis has brought about tears, eye-opening moments, battles with schools and mostly internal battles within myself as I have learned how to fight for my family. I know that so many families struggle with issues like this and my prayer is that my journey, lessons learned and wisdom gained will come through as I share my heart with you through the pages of this book! God has also taught me about finding rest in the busyness of life; saying "no" to a lot and to be okay with being at peace. It's been a challenge and a learning curve for me but it's been the most revealing, revolutionary season of my life. God always has us endure things so that we can help others. I cannot wait to share what I've learned with you. I also found out I was pregnant with our fifth child, which was both exciting, scary and eye-opening. This child has already taught me how to listen to my body, how to truly rest and how to

find joy and contentment in life. For my precious son, Baker, because normal is over-rated.

OVERRATED

A Christian woman's guide to living authentically in a perfection-driven world.

Ashley Schubert

Author of:

Raising a Business and Babies

30 Days to Shine

Brittanie Ebrite: Editor

Hilarie Salamone: Cover Design

Y'all Are Crazy Publishing LLC

CHAPTERS

Chapter 1: Normal
Chapter 2: Shiny Floors
Chapter 3: Excuses
Chapter 4: Busyness
Chapter 5: Comparison
Chapter 6: Waiting
Chapter 7: Others' Opinions
Chapter 8: Perfection

CHAPTER 1: NORMAL

And we know that in all things, God works for the good of those who love him, who have been called according to his purpose. Romans 8:28

"GOD DOES HIS BEST MIRACLES IN OUR BIGGEST MESSES." - PASTOR STEVEN FURTICK

GOAL OF THIS CHAPTER: LETTING GO OF "NORMAL" IN YOUR VOCABULARY, MIND AND THE WAY YOU LIVE!

What the heck does normal mean anyway? Well, according to the Cambridge dictionary, it means "conforming to a standard; usual; typical or expected." When you put it that way, who wants to be normal anyway? When did we decide it was a good idea to all be the same, behave the same and turn out the same as everyone else? When did we start letting society tell us that we, or our kids, are not going to be successful just because we don't conform or aren't typical. Normal is out and uniqueness is in! I certainly don't want my kids to feel like they have to conform in order to be accepted, loved and valuable. I want to model for them that it's okay to create your own version of normal, each and every day.

This chapter has been the hardest one I've ever had to write. Just writing the dedication of this book brings tears to my eyes. I'm not a crier. Not in any sense. But when it comes to my children – my child, and his future, as I'm sure any Mom can understand, my feelings begin to emerge.

Kids with photos of perfect smiles, poses and neatly tucked-in shirts at all times are over-rated.

If you see any picture on social media, my kids are often naked, barefoot and covered in mud. That's because, at our house, we believe in playing outside and in getting dirty. Don't get me wrong, they dress up for church on Sundays in dresses and polo shirts and they wear uniforms to school each day. Their hair is brushed and they look nice when they need to look nice. But, when they are home, we let them be kids.

I have plenty of friends who will cringe when they see photos of my kids covered with mud from head-to-toe. And that's totally okay. My vision for a happy home may not be theirs and theirs is not mine. We don't have to agree on the way we choose to raise our kiddos but we can respect each other's parenting choices and laugh at each other when our kids do something silly.

If your kids need a bath at the end of each day, that's a sign that they had a great day! If they need more than one bath a day, even better! When my babies are little, say two or under, I love nothing more than giving them a bath in the kitchen sink. There is nothing better than putting that squishy baby in the sink and filling it up with warm, sudsy water. It brings me back to an older time, a time when that was the normal thing to do. It makes me feel like I am living decades ago and bathing my baby in the only place that made sense. In our new house, I had a new sink installed. A big, single basin white sink and I had one stipulation - make sure it's big enough I can bathe my baby in it. That sounds funny but it's amazing! I love my big sink and I'll relish these special moments!

A Goal Worth Having

Having clean kids is not a goal worthy of attaining. Be free to let your kids play outside, get dirty and let yourself laugh when they enjoy playing in the mud. Consider it an accomplishment when they need a bath at the end of each night! That means they had a fun day and you are a great mom!

==OVERRATED==

==Having happy kids, well-adjusted kids, polite kids, thankful kids and thoughtful kids is a goal worth having.== How can we ensure our kids will develop these characteristics we want them to have?

1. Speak positivity over your kids and call out the gifts you see in them. Kindness, intelligence, athleticism, friendliness, attention to detail, leadership. All of these things can be apparent in children and can be helpful to call out in them as they grow. People can become who you tell them they are. Children are no different.
2. Actions speak so loud. Model for your kids what you want them to do and how you want them to behave. Be kind to people, thoughtful and polite. Your kids will be watching.
3. Be thankful and inspire a home of thankfulness. Go around the table each night and say the things you are thankful for or what was the best part of your day. Let your kids take part in this and determine what they should say.
4. Provide a safe, nourishing environment full of hugs and plenty of love. Kids want to feel safe and known.
5. Let them be kids. Playing outside, laughing, playing make-believe, kids need this! And frankly, they don't need you watching their every move. Give yourself the freedom to let them play and imagine with their siblings or alone without you present. Watch their imaginations soar.

Your Kid Is The Only One

When my third child started preschool, we went through some really tough days. I was getting calls from his principal and teachers daily and their words were less than encouraging. One of them told me "Your son is the only one in the class who is not normal." Talk about breaking a momma's heart. That was a rough day and I cried several times. I want to share with you the entry I wrote down in my journal that day. It's pretty raw but it's how I felt in that time:

I will be your advocate. I will fight for you no matter what. I'll be your biggest fan and no one will love you more than me. No matter what it takes, we will get you on course and help you every step along the way. I won't give up even if I have to fight alone. I will let your smile and good days push me, even on the bad days. We will get through. I'll be there for you, loving you and standing beside you, celebrating you, your differences and all. And we will succeed, you will succeed, my sweet boy.

Since then, we were introduced to an occupational therapist and she helps my son two days a week before school. You see, we have learned that he has Sensory Processing Issues, or Sensory Integration. He doesn't process things the way most kids do and he gets overstimulated easily. Once I learned to understand this and start approaching him differently and treating him as unique, it made things so much better for our family. Finally, I understood him and what he needed. There are still rough days and he has hard days at school occasionally. He also has really great days and I can see his sweet smile and personality shine through and it melts my heart.

I shared this story with one of our pastors and he said to me "Who wants their children to be normal anyway?" He went on to say "Normal means they are living in a way that the world approves of. It means fitting in and going with the crowd. Normal is "overrated". Wow! When I started thinking of things from this angle, it totally changed my perspective! All I wanted was for my son to be normal, to fit in, to not stand out! In reality, don't we want our kids to stand out, have their own personalities and live in the spirit God created them to live? Yes! It's just tough to embrace the abnormal and the difficult circumstances that we must endure by having a child who the world treats differently. Take heart! God created your child in the way he did for a reason, for a purpose. It's our jobs, as moms, to call out their gifts in them and lead them in the right path!

When Normal is Boring

Do you know what is considered normal? Pretty much everything I am against. I basically spend my life making my own path and not worrying about what society sees as normal. So, why would I expect my children to fit in, to conform and say "yes" to everything and to fit into a box. Boxes are boring, and you guessed it, normal is overrated. I want to teach my children to be confident in making their own decisions, and to stick by those decisions. I want them to pursue dreams because God put them in their hearts and gave them special abilities. I don't know what they will be someday but I pray they will each use their gifts for God's glory.

Here are some "normal" things that have never appealed to me: forever homes (Where is the fun in that, right?!), spotless kids (Let them be kids!), binging and laying on the couch all weekend (Set some goals!), being consumed with busyness and wearing it as a trophy (Set your priorities, girl!). We will discuss many of these in the chapters ahead and go deeper into how to get past these crutches. The point is, create your own normal and don't feel like you must fit into a box. You shouldn't and neither should your children. Happiness begins when you decide to stop needing the validation of others.

Every time I would pick Baker up from school and the teacher would tell me he had a hard day, I would feel like a failure as a parent. I would internalize the guilt which was not fair or healthy. As we progressed through school and therapy, I learned to let it roll off, give it to God and trust that we were all doing our best. It helped tremendously as there were continually good days and bad days.

Through A Childs' Eyes

Have you ever looked at an adventure through a child's eyes? The great thing about kids is this, they are amazed easily! Kids find the joy in any situation and enjoy it! We can learn a lot from our kids. I believe that's why Jesus said "Unless you have faith like a child you will never enter the kingdom of God". Jesus knew that childlike faith is hard for adults. We are much more difficult to impress and we want to see proof before believing. When did we lose that childlike faith?

My kids can have fun doing the simplest things. Playing in the mud, collecting sticks and rocks outside, playing with a balloon. It's funny to observe! They can laugh and enjoy life when we are doing the most normal tasks. It's fantastic and they always make me laugh.

Let's look at life through a child's eyes. Let's be intentional about finding the fun and the joy in the simple things. Of course, those things are going to look different for us. Maybe the little things for an adult are enjoying the warm sunshine on our shoulders, sipping a cup of hot coffee in the mornings, reading a good book before bed.

I used to watch "I Love Lucy" a lot in junior high, high school and college. I have every DVD ever made (truth). I even decorated my college dorm room in "I Love Lucy" memorabilia (don't judge!). You cannot watch this show without laughing. Now, I miss that laughter and anytime I need a good laugh, I can pull out one of those movies and laugh my head off once again! Laughter is good for the soul.

No No No to Anxiety

Do you know what else is considered normal? Anxiety and stress. Women have it. Women are consumed with it. They tell us to live with it and deal with it. A friend once asked me how I seem to be at peace with anxiety. The truth is that I have never felt it. Nervousness, yes. Overwhelmed, yes. Anxious, yes. But I can honestly say that I've never felt anxiety. I'm not trying to say I'm brave or great or above that. It's just that I learned at an early age to let a lot of things go, trust in God and not worry about being perfect. Thankfully, I believe my mom instilled a lot of this into me. Thanks, Mom!

Saying no to anxiety is a daily choice for many, I get that. Finding ways to relieve anxiety is important and worth exploring. What does it mean for you? Consider what makes you feel better and how you can do more of that! Also consider what triggers the anxiety and work to avoid it. Anxiety sucks. And it's time to get it under control, Sister. And then you can teach your daughters and friends not to let it consume them either.

Take each day to learn and grow and really flourish where you are, even on those days ridden with fear and the unknown. This normal doesn't have to be your norm.

Saying No to Normal

I've decided that I will no longer be bogged down by what is expected and anticipated to be true.

I've given up on saying yes on things beyond my control.

I will not be pushed into feeling things that are untrue.

I will not be told that my child must fit into a box. Because you know what? Who wants to live inside of a box anyway?

Boxes are stuffy, confined, predictable and well...brown. I want my child to have adventure, embrace uniqueness and let his personality shine! I'll find joy in the uncommon, the weird, the life lessons we learn along the way.

I'll take all the hugs I'm given. The "I love you's" along the way. I'll be proud throughout this journey. I'm determined to find the joy in each day!

Ashley Schubert, 2020

In what ways can you embrace your child (grandchild, family member or friend) that is not considered normal?

_____
_____

In what ways do you want what's considered "normal" to not be the norm in your own life?

_____
_____

CHAPTER 2: SHINY FLOORS

Above all, put on love - the perfect bond of unity. Colossians 3:14

"GOD ABSOLUTELY LOVES TO TAKE ORDINARY PEOPLE AND DO EXTRAORDINARY THINGS IN THEM, THROUGH THEM, AND WITH THEM." - LYSA TERKEURST

GOAL OF THE CHAPTER: REALIZING THAT YOU CAN STILL HAVE A CLEAN, INVITING AND LIFE-GIVING HOME, EVEN WITHOUT THE SHINY FLOORS.

If your floors are shiny and spotless, I'm envious of you. No, seriously, someday I want to be like you. But today, I'm not, and I'm so glad my floors have some crumbs and some sticky juice-spilled stains. It's a sign of life, of living, of fun. You see, shiny floors are for those who have lives that don't involve children running everywhere and mud being tracked in. Don't get me wrong, I love a clean house! I vacuum regularly and my house is most always picked up. I like it to look clutter-free and welcoming! But my floors are seldom sparkling. Except for the day my cleaning lady comes over and mops them with that amazing smelling cleaner! They just won't stay sparkling for more than that one day! They will find new ones to get stained and sticky. I will wipe up spills and clean up crumbs and fingerprints.

I also know that one day I will miss this. I will miss those fingerprints and messy floors. I will miss all the laundry and the cookie crumbs. Yes, I will, even on days when that seems very unlikely.

ASHLEY SCHUBERT

Rarely a day goes by that my house isn't loud, messy and crazy! I mean, I currently have 4 kids under 7 for Pete's sake. It's just the season I am in. If I'm being honest, sometimes it's hard to be joyful amongst the chaos. The noise gets so loud, it's so constant and it feels like a never-ending cycle of everyone needing me all the time. It's not really about balance. It's about finding a rhythm, a harmony that works. It's about letting go of what we think our life is supposed to look like. It's about letting go of what others lives look like from the outside looking in. It's about embracing the mess and truly finding joy, even in the midst of the chaos.

I could have chosen to have a clean and tidy house, my house, without a husband and without a houseful of kids. It could have been tidy and beautiful with everything in its place. Everything could smell nice and be shiny, but that was never my goal. My goal was to have a houseful of kids and with that comes noise, mud and laughter. So I get to clean up messes, put things back in their place over and over again and I work hard to keep my house tidy. But it's worth it. Even if the floors aren't always shiny.

Nothin' Gonna Steal My Joy

There ain't nothing gonna steal my joy. Yeah, there ain't nothing gonna steal my joy. We sing that as we drive home from work or even as we wake up in the mornings and get ready for the day. In those moments, all is calm and everyone is happy and we are at peace. Reality sets in as soon as we transition into the next thing. For me, it often happens on the weekend when I arrive home after an afternoon of working, feeling rejuvenated and optimistic. I drive home ready to see my family. I've only been away 2-3 hours and I usually schedule it so the little ones will be napping while I'm gone. I'm signing this song as it plays the radio, determined to be filled with joy through the rest of the day. And then I walk into the house.

Inevitably, the house is a mess! Toys are scattered around, food and cups are lying on the table, the kids are either loud or totally lethargic and plated in front of the tv. My husband is rested and setting in the chair, relaxed after an afternoon of reading and a nap, while the kids destroyed the house. He doesn't have a care in the world. I am silently fuming. "Why couldn't he make sure the house is clean?" "Why aren't the kids playing outside and enjoying the day?" "How does he feel good napping so easily when I always have a full plate?" All good questions, but they're not productive. They definitely will not help me keep my joy.

What would be more productive is to be happy that I have a husband who loves our kids and who is able to be home with them. I can be thankful that we have a nice house and things to fill it. It doesn't mean I shouldn't speak to my husband about this at a later time, when I'm not upset, and let him know what could be done differently to help out (which I do!).

What we allow our mind to consume, believe and dwell on becomes our mood. Our mood becomes our outlook and our outlook becomes our heart.

Sticky Floors, Clean House

This is not an excuse to be messy and have a dirty house. Even as busy moms, we can keep a home that we can be proud of and enjoy! I have learned some practical tips that help me keep my house generally clean overall.

1. Make your bed each day.
2. Pick up toys, stuff, papers, etc. at the end of each day so you can start fresh!
3. Start the dishwasher each night or morning!
4. Teach your kids to clean up at the end of each day.
5. Do the laundry from start to finish- wash, dry, fold, put up.

None of these are easy. Trust me, I know. None of them are fun, necessarily. But the more you do them, the more routine they become and the easier it will be to get into a rhythm. Doing these things will help make your life simpler and leave you feeling a sigh of relief at the end of each day!

Hiring a cleaning service is an excellent way to ensure your home gets deep cleaned regularly. I currently use this service twice per month. It ensures my floors get mopped, toilets and showers get scrubbed and everything is fully cleaned for me. I used to only do this twice a year, and then I went to once a quarter and then once a month. Do what works for you! It's a wonderful feeling to come home to a clean house that you didn't have to clean. Money well spent!

An Unlikely Friendship

We got invited to go to the park with a friend this week. Not so much a friend as an acquaintance. Our kids go to school together but we know nothing about each other's families and have never spent time together. I agreed to the play date not knowing what I was getting myself into! This mom was basically the complete opposite of me. Poised, quiet, totally a rule-follower and very structured. She has one daughter and their life is very planned, packed full of activities that will enrich her social and academic skills, with clean clothes and perfectly braided hair. And then you have my children. In case you have never gone to the park with us, let me give you a visual of what you would see. We come bounding out of the car, with Chick-Fil-A in hand. The kids are all dressed but the boys clothes definitely don't match. My second son has on a pair of mud boots (there is no rain or mud in sight). The baby has a ketchup stain on his sweatshirt because he got a little excited about eating those waffle fries and dipping excessively in his new favorite food group, ketchup. My daughter's hair is not fixed but it might be brushed (maybe), as long as she did it herself in the car on the way there. And then there is me. I'm in leggings, a t-shirt and tennis shoes. I have a baby carrier hanging off me, two bags dangling from my shoulder and a drink carrier in one hand. I'm sure that mom wondered what she had gotten herself into when she showed up and saw us. The first thing my oldest son did was historical yet totally normal in our house! He said "Mom, I need to pee". Without missing a beat, I said "go over there behind that tree". He took off running and dropped his pants behind that tree and did his pee-pee business. That mom looked at me like I had lost my mind. I realized right then and there that we were not destined to be besties. The rest of the day went about the same way. The boys chased each other with sticks, chased her daughter with sticks and acted like dinosaurs getting dirty and growling. She continued to look at me with odd stares and confusion. At the end of the day, we parted ways with smiles, probably both thinking "well that was...interesting".

Situations like this have shown me that in these cases, we can either adapt to make someone else more comfortable or we can be ourselves and be proud of that. I decided to go for the latter. So what if my boys pee behind trees? So, what if they play with sticks and growl at each other pretending to be dinosaurs? They are kids and they are mine. I'm glad they know how to pee outside and use their imaginations playing together. I'm glad they love the outdoors and feel comfortable playing with sticks and getting dirty. But that's just me.

I'm sure she is proud her daughter likes to stay clean and polished. I'm sure she is proud to take her to all the activities to keep her busy and active. That's her and that's what makes her and her family happy, I hope.

We are all different and we are raising our families differently. It doesn't mean we can't be friends. It just means we may not be best matched to be best friends and share our lives together. And that's totally okay. As long as we can respect each other, say hello and smile and understand that we are both unique, that's totally okay.

Less Is More

The more kids I have, the harder it is to keep the clutter down and the more time it requires of me to clean and organize. I also become more and more into "less and less". Decluttering brings me joy, I like putting things in bags and boxes to give away, and when I clean out my kids' toy boxes, I feel a thrill! This has not always been the case, but it's come with time and practice.

Just like my closet, I clean out my kids' toys, my cabinets and my drawers quarterly. I throw away things that haven't been used in the past quarter or I move it to the front and give it one more chance. If it hasn't been used by the end of the next quarter, I then say "bye-bye" and into the giveaway box it goes! Pro tip: Always clean out your kids' toy boxes when they are not around. If they see you doing it, they will not want to give anything away and you'll end up keeping way more than you need to! Here is a guideline for keeping toys:

1. Is it broken? -If yes, TOSS.
2. Do they still play with it? - If no, donate it.
3. Can it be passed down to a younger sibling? -If yes, keep or store it.
4. Is it in good condition and do they play with it regularly? -If yes and yes, keep it!

This same rule will apply to your closet as well. Follow these guidelines:

1. Have I worn it in this last season? -If no, donate.
2. Does it have rips or stains? -If yes, TOSS.
3. Do I wear it regularly and still love it? -If yes, keep it!

When it comes to decorating, keeping things de-cluttered looks and feels so much better than over doing things ever will. As a realtor, I see inside a lot of homes! The ones that draw the eye the most and convey a sense of comfort are the ones that are clean, smell good and de-cluttered. Instead of filling your home with more and more, consider filling it with more that matters. Here are some ideas:

1. Hang up or set out photos of family (other than your own children). Use photos of grandparents, great-grandparents, aunts and uncles and be proud of the black-and-whites. Show your children their heritage and be proud of it!
2. Use creams and white as a baseline and then throw in pops of color that inspire you!
3. Displays items that mean something and tell a story.
4. Books are a great way to showcase places you have been, things you love and conversation starters.

How To Be The Hostess Without the Stress

I love throwing parties and having get-together at my home. I love bringing people together and planning events. What I don't love is the stress that people try to bring into it. Here's the thing, you don't have to have a party that stresses you out.

I used to get stressed at my kids' parties for many reasons. Some family was always late, someone didn't really want to be there, there were complaints about my food selection and the list goes on! I was so worried about pleasing others that I didn't get to enjoy my kids' parties. That's not fair to them or to me! Now I've learned to do things differently so that the days are more enjoyable:

1. Serve food on paper plates.
2. Use minimal decorations.
3. Buy the cake if you don't like, or have time, for baking.
4. Send invitations electronically so you don't have to buy paper ones.
5. Just enjoy the moment! Don't worry about having everything on the table, everything looking perfect and all the guests being comfortable. That's where the stress comes in. It's more important to enjoy the event, enjoy the mo-

ment and let everyone get what they need if they need it.

Be more focused on making your home a place of safety, love and comfort. Don't worry about making it a place of perfection. Keep your home clean and tidy but realize that fingerprints are going to happen and mud is going to get tracked in. Enjoy your home, love it and if you don't, make it what you love or find a new one. Maybe that's just the realtor in me talking!

Make a Game Plan
When I was thrown into a crazy world of homeschooling that I never signed up for, during the disaster of the Coronavirus (more on this in a later chapter), I realized that I would need a plan to keep our whole family on track. Not only did I still have to maintain my current workload. I also had to help my kids with their schoolwork each day to ensure they got it all done. I made sure they were on all their video conferences with their teachers so that we finished out the remaining eight weeks of the semester. On top of that, I had to make sure we were eating well, exercising daily and that my kids were learning basic life skills and they were being fed spiritually each day.

Here is the schedule I developed:

Schubert Spring Schedule 2020

7:30-8:00 - Wake Up & Relax - Mom Devotional

8:00-8:30 - Breakfast, get dressed & make beds!

8:30-8:45 - Bible Lesson & songs

8:45-11:00 - Learning Time

Bowen Classroom (Big Computer) Brylee- (iPad in Room- IXL, Reading, Book Reports) Baker & Benaiah (Living Room/Playroom) - Blocks, Puzzles, Books & Cards

11:00-12:00 - FREE TIME TOGETHER - OUTSIDE

12:00-1:00 - LUNCH & FREE TIME (Mom Works)

1:00-2:30 - Learning Time & Benaiah Nap

Bowen Classroom (Big Computer) Brylee- (iPad in Room- IXL, Reading, Book Reports) Baker- Learning in Dining Room & Rest Time

2:30-4:00 - SNACK & FREE TIME (Mom Works)

4:00-5:00 - Exercise Together

5:00-6:00 - Mom Cooks/Works & Kids Play

6:00-8:00 - Supper & Family Time

8:00-8:30 - Bath & BED

It's seriously the only way my family was able to survive each day and make sure we checked off everything on our list! It helped my children feel a sense of security because they knew what to expect next. I built in time for our spiritual life, as well as exercise and play time! It was important for me to give them several times of "free time" during the day too because I wanted them to learn to make their own decisions and not be told what to do all the time. They often used this free time to play outside, play a game or watch a video on their iPads or even watch a tv show. It's their free time and their choice! As long as they are getting everything else done, I'm happy!

This schedule will look different this summer and for each new season. Yours will most definitely look different for your family! It's a framework to build around to ensure things stay together, get accomplished and everything is being fulfilled. Each day, I prayed for God to give me wisdom, patience and strength to be who I needed to be!

Just Begin

Don't be so focused on things being perfect in order to start, that you forget to start.

Don't be so worried about things being perfect in order to take the first step, that you don't take a step at all.

Don't stress about all the details so much, that there are no details to attend to later.

Just begin. Make a plan. Start where you are.

Ashley Schubert, 2020

What can you do to make your home a place where others can feel loved, welcomed and accepted?

_____
_____

Do you need to develop a schedule in your home? Start with: 1) What needs to be accomplished? 2) Time block how long each step will take. 3) Build in spiritual/physical needs! 4) Add free

time!

_____
_____
_____
_____

CHAPTER 3: EXCUSES

Whatever you do, in word or deed, do everything in the name of the Lord Jesus, giving thanks to God the Father through Him. 1 Colossians 3:17

"GOD IS ALREADY IN MY TOMORROW." - PASTOR STEVEN FURTICK

GOAL OF THE CHAPTER: LETTING GO OF EXCUSES ONCE AND FOR ALL, SO YOU CAN MOVE FORWARD AND SUCCEED!

For some reason, when God calls me to write a book, I begin to feel totally unqualified to write about the topic he gives me. Even if in the past I have felt totally ready and capable of writing on the topic. I begin to doubt myself and the doubt begins to creep in. I am learning that it's just part of the writing process. The enemy wants me to stop, to quit and to make excuses. The enemy wants me to disqualify myself. But the truth is, I was never really qualified. I am only able because God has qualified me.

If y'all know me, you know that excuses are my Achilles heel. Like, I cannot stand them. Don't give me excuses unless it's a darn good one. In the business world, it's so common to hear excuses: I'm sick, I'm too busy, it's Spring break/Fall break, Christmas break, Summer break and the list goes on! Here is the truth, we all have the same 24 hours in each day. It's what we do with them that counts!

Excuses are useless. They are a myth. And they can be overcome! Instead of making an excuse, think about doing what you need to do ANYWAY. But it's a lot of work? Do it ANYWAY. The task looks daunting? Do it ANYWAY. It's sure to be draining. Do it ANYWAY.

I wish I could say this loudly so you could hear my intensity and how much I believe in this. These three words can change your life. DO IT ANYWAY.

Just do it. Nike coined this phrase and it's been a good one for their brand. When you hear those three words, you instantly associate them with Nike. Maybe you should also associate them with your life. When it's hard, it's late, it's exhausting, it's overwhelming... just do it.

My Number is 3

If you have never taken the Enneagram, I highly recommend you do. It's a personality test and it gives you a number that tells about your personality and highlights your strengths and weaknesses. It really helps to understand yourself better and your motivations. My number is 3: the Achiever. Here is an overview of my personality type, as per Enneagram Explorations:

You want to be competent, productive, accomplished and dynamic. More importantly, you want to be good at what you do and to look good doing it. You see yourself as ambitious, competitive and industrious. Your idealized image is that you are triumphant and victorious. You are goal oriented. To say you are self-confident, ambitious and motivated may be an understatement.

NEED: You need to be the best at whatever you do. You love the sound of applause and accolades for a job well done.

AVOID: You avoid failure, nothingness, being second best or appearing like you cannot accomplish what is expected of you.

VICE: You may feel like you always have to greet the world with a smile so people will smile at you.

Wing: Type 3 with the 2 Wing: You see yourself as supportive, caring, cheerful, fun and friendly.

Wow! I feel like I just let you into my inner world, my mind and my feelings. You know me a little better. Maybe you can relate to his personality type? Maybe it is yours too or maybe it's totally off base for you and you don't relate at all. That's okay! I encourage you to take the test yourself and figure out your number. It will truly help you understand yourself better.

Here's what's crazy about being a number 3. Yes, I achieve a lot because I'm driven to constantly be achieving. People say "That's amazing! You are wired to achieve." While it is a blessing, it's also a thorn in my side. Because I am wired this way, I am also wired to feel like a failure if I'm not achieving and not checking things off my list. I tell you this to tell you that we all have strengths and weaknesses. A lot of times, our strengths are also our weaknesses.

Strengths and Weaknesses

I asked my Circle Group of women to identify their top strength and top weakness. For many, they discovered they are one in the same. It was a good exercise to help the women see what they think about themselves, how they feel about themselves and how to relate to their friend sitting beside them. So many said my strength is (this) and it's also my weakness. It's a catch-22.

I can relate to that. My strength of being driven and wanting to get things done is also a detriment. Being that I want to check off boxes, it makes me skip over details. I am so far from a perfectionist! I don't care how great it looks or if it all adds up and the details are perfect. I just want to get it done. I see this in my oldest son, who is 5. He is so much like me! That's why I can relate so well to him. He goes fast at everything and doesn't care about the details, often skipping over little things. It drives his Dad crazy! He is the opposite of us. Isn't it funny how we see ourselves in our kids! We see this all the time and it's hilarious and eye-opening!

What are your strengths and weaknesses? This is a great exercise to do with your family, at your office, with your church group, etc. It will make you take a closer look into yourself and into your friends. Write these things down and think about how you can improve in both areas.

Hot or Cold?

Have you seen the movie "War Room"? If you haven't, it's a fantastic movie and you should watch it now! Once you do, you will totally understand this scene I'm about to tell you about. The scene involves an old woman, probably in her 80s, but she is spry, feisty and ornery. She wants to sell her house and invites over a realtor to help her. This realtor is a younger woman, married with a family, who is having problems in her marriage and struggling to find peace in her life. The older woman, Miss Clara, asks the young woman how her walk with God is going. She asks if she goes to church and tries to dig deeper into her spiritual life but the young woman isn't giving answers easily. Instead, she says "It's fine, we believe, we love God but we don't really have time to go to church or live fully committed to Him". Miss Clara shakes her head and goes to grab some coffee from the kitchen for both of them. She returns and hands one to her young friend who takes a sip. "Miss Clara, you like your coffee room temperature?" She asked with a confused look. Miss Clara replies "No, Honey, I like mine HOT!" She goes on to say "People either like their coffee hot or cold, but no one likes it lukewarm." God is the same way. He either wants his people on fire for Him or we are just cold. Being lukewarm doesn't help anyone, including ourselves.

How do you feel like you are in each area of your life? Are you hot, cold or just lukewarm?

At Home (With your family, spouse, kids)
At Work (With your drive, co-workers, success)
Spiritual Relationship (Prayer life, Bible reading, Church)
Physical (Working out regularly, stretching, drinking water)

These areas are all important if we want to have full and fulfilling lives. If we aren't hot in them, then we might as well be cold. Being lukewarm doesn't help anyone and it certainly doesn't help yourself. Amen and amen.

How to live HOT at HOME:

Make family time a priority

Make a schedule

Show plenty of love

How to live HOT at WORK:

Use your planner

Set goals

Be driven.

How to live HOT in your Spiritual Life:

Reading your Bible, devotional or even your Bible app each morning is a great way to start each day. It's also a great way to end each day. Make your method of choice easily accessible and visible so you start each day with it a priority!

Pray throughout the day and not just at planned times. We always pray with the kids before meals and before bed. That's the rule, the law, the way we live. They now know that's what we do and they never question it. It's just as important to pray throughout the day, to have an open and honest line of communication with God at all times.

Going to church should not be an option, it should be a priority. Whether you feel like going or not, whether your kids want to go or not, whether it's cold or hot or raining or you would rather be at the lake, go to church. Of course, there will be times of vacation or illness or times when you are not available. But, those times should be few and church must be a priority. I'm speaking the truth and I'm speaking boldly.

How to live HOT with your Health:

I bought a gallon-size water jug recently. It tracks how much water I'm drinking and keeps me accountable. Let me tell you, I am a terrible water drinker. This giant thing looks funny to carry around (and it's really heavy at the beginning of the day). However, I am drinking a full gallon of water every day! Plus a cup of coffee in the morning and a cup of hot tea at night and usually a few drinks in between at lunch and supper time. I've never drank this much in my life! I feel better and I know my body feels better too.

I have never been a huge workout fanatic. But I have always done something to stay in shape. My husband is an Exercise Science major and has a huge passion for fitness. I don't live for the gym but I do believe very strongly in staying healthy and strong! For me, that means doing a walk every day, moving my body, and being active. It usually means a walk outside every day and in the cold weather, it means going to the gym and getting my activity in there! No excuses, health is so important and we only get one body in this life!

I had four babies and didn't see the chiropractor much during that time. About a year after I had my fourth, I started having some tension in my upper back and neck. If you know me or see my pictures, I'm most often seeing carrying or wearing a baby (or two!) so it's no surprise. I went in and she examined me. She said "Well you have 8 ribs out and your pelvis is twisted like a corkscrew." Wonderful! She adjusted me and I decided I better start going regularly to keep my body in check. This was a wake-up call to me. I was living with a severely misaligned body and wasn't taking time to think about my health. This was a problem. It was time to make a change. I started going regularly and putting it on my calendar to make sure it got done. This can be applicable to any healthcare professional that you need to be seeing. Your health should be a top priority, even when we, as women, tend to put ourselves last so often.

I used to get a massage once a year. It was most often a Mother's Day gift card that I would receive and feel like it was okay to spend that time on myself. Now, I go every other month. I have finally allowed myself to feel like I deserved it, to not feel bad about taking care of myself and yes, even pampering myself. Now, I make appointments and make myself a priority, and that includes all areas of my health.

The Mindset Shift of Money

We all know about budgeting, paying with cash, not overspending and living within our means. In our culture, being broke becomes a staple, a norm, and I'm telling you right now, it doesn't have to be this way. You want to see the change? Be the change.

Do what it takes to get your family out of debt if that's the case. Save, save, save. And then invest. Save and invest. Pay your bills, save and invest. This is definitely a mindset shift and it takes dedication and a strong desire. Especially if you are changing your family tree, but it's worth it!

"Just do what you love" is a common phrase that is thrown around in our culture. This is a silly thing that someone once said to make people think they can just do whatever makes them happy and all will be well. Happiness is one thing. Your security, bank account and future are another. How about instead of just doing what we love, we do something we love that provides us with a good income? How about we teach our kids about paychecks, taxes and real life instead of just encouraging "do what makes you happy."?

When you find your passion, when you know your why and when you find a dream that allows you to make a good income for your family, that's the sweet spot. Find that! Do everything you can to find that! You'll know you're in your sweet spot when it comes easily to you, when you enjoy what you're doing, when it's fun and when it allows you to make a good income. That's where it all aligns and that's when you can make strides.

Graphic Tees

Graphic tees are everywhere these days. And for women, they get a little out of control. You've seen the ones I'm talking about. "Feed me tacos and tell me I'm pretty", "Rose All Day", "I don't wake up until noon". I'm not sure where all these came from and they sure are funny. But are they what we want to be known for? When we really think about the meanings behind these things, are they true for how we feel about ourselves? I hope not! Watch the video by comedian John Crist, where he talks about the silliness of graphic tees! Like, he says "Your Grandfather fought in World War II and you can't 'adult' today?" It's funny and I crack up anytime I hear him talk about this. And then I get a little sad because our society is seriously becoming weak in many areas.

Let's get some graphic tees with inspiring messages! Here are a few that I have:

Coffee, Pray, Conquer
Living on a Prayer
Mom Life is the Best Life
Everything I Touch Turns to Sold
Chaos Coordinator
Not Today, Satan

These are some of my favorites because they are true and they also exemplify joy and positivity. You are what you wear and how you portray yourself. Let's portray ourselves as bold, positive and joyful! We will start believing that about ourselves too!

Take Mine

Take my busyness and turn it into productivity.

Take my to-do list and make it yours.

Take my overwhelmed spirit and help me to grant grace.

Take my trophies and use them for your purpose.

ASHLEY SCHUBERT

Take my weariness and give me true rest.

Oh, Lord, may your ways always overtake mine.

Ashley Schubert, 2019

How can you eliminate excuses in your life?

CHAPTER 4: BUSYNESS

The Lord bless you and keep you; the Lord make His face shine on you and be gracious to you; the Lord turn His face toward you and give you peace. Numbers 6:24-26

"WOMEN WHO SAY YES TO GOD WILL SEE LIFE LIKE FEW OTHERS."
-LYSA TERKEURST

GOAL OF THE CHAPTER: SAYING GOODBYE TO BUSYNESS AND YES TO YOUR BEST LIFE!

I had a stirring to list our house, the house that we had only lived in for 3 years, the house that we loved. It had it all: the land, the trees, the space for the kids to run and the beauty inside. We had put in a lot of work outside to make it how we wanted it to be, a place where we could enjoy and we could host. At this house, we had hosted numerous gatherings, cookouts, parties, even a wedding for my sister-in-law. It was "the house" and no one could believe that we wanted to move. But we did and we listed the house that week. We had over a dozen showings, lots of interest and it looked amazing. And then something surreal happened, we decided to stay. As a realtor, I never encourage people to list their house and then take it off the market. I don't recommend it or want anyone to set out to do it. However, listing my own home, I made the decision to do it and here is why. Through this process, we realized just how special our place truly was. We saw our place in a new light. We saw the beauty and we realized just how blessed we are to own a place like this.

We decided to make some improvements to help us stay in our home and make it better. I had my kitchen painted white and it brightened it up instantly! It suddenly became the kitchen I had always wanted. It had been on my goals list and I was finally able to check it off! We added fencing around our pond to make it safer for the kids. We spruced everything up and I decluttered the inside and donated everything we no longer used. I repainted our playroom and arranged things properly. I now love our home more than ever. That time of listing our home was not a waste. It was God teaching me to see the beauty in our season, to truly love our space and to appreciate it each and every day. It allowed me to make the improvements I had wanted to make for years. It gave us new eyes, new appreciation and a new love for right where we were, right where we still are. We only had to sit down, cut down on the noise and busyness and listen. Let God speak and see the beauty within.

The definition of overrated according to Merriam-Webster is "Rated or valued too highly". If you ask anyone how their day is going or how their year has been, they will likely reply with "busy", "we're so busy". Busyness has become a badge of honor, something for us to be proud to say. But, why is that the case? Why are we so proud of our busyness? I believe we feel we need to be busy or to be viewed as busy so that we feel successful or like we are valuable.

The Season of No

In 2019, I started to feel a sense of overwhelm with too much on my plate, for the first time ever. Sure, I had 4 babies in 6 years, started a new business from scratch, wrote a book and balanced all the things in between. And maybe that was the problem. It all started catching up and all of a sudden, I felt God calling me to live a life filled with more peace. I decided that in 2020, it was going to be my "season of no".

I created an image in my mind and decided that if things did not fit in the image, the answer would be no. These were my 6 areas I wanted to focus fully on for the year ahead:

FAITH
FAMILY/FRIENDS
BUSINESS
WRITING/SPEAKING
HEALTH
HOME

This may sound harsh or intense but you have to understand me to understand this life shift. As I said in a previous chapter, I am a number 3, the "achiever"/"performer" on the Enneagram test. My whole life has been filled with the need to constantly achieve which meant never taking a day off, saying yes to everything and always feeling the need to lead. This comes with great benefits in that I was able to escalate my career quickly, out work most anyone in my field and accomplish more than the average woman. It also becomes a thorn in my side often. As great as accomplishing can be, it's also filled with a need for more and never feeling "enough". Yikes!

I found myself working too many hours a week, constantly juggling work with my life and on top of that, leading two groups at my church and being the leader in every group I was a part of. I could never be content in just being part of a group. I always had to be leading the group, which meant constant planning, preparing and taking on everyone else's needs. I was doing all this on auto-pilot without even realizing the stress I was putting on myself.

By saying no to some things that did not fit into one of these areas, I freed myself up to say YES to things that would truly have an impact!

What are some areas where you want to focus on right now?

1.
2.

3.
4.
5.

Feel free to add more, or maybe you only need to write down 3! That's okay. Give yourself grace in this. Now, when things come along and you need to say YES or NO, see if it happens to fall into one of these areas. If the answer is no, just say NO and move forward with confidence knowing that you have freed yourself up to YES to something else, something better!

The Season of Blah

After finding out I was pregnant with our fifth child, I went through the normal first trimester feelings: nausea, exhaustedness (Is that a word?) and just feelings of "blah". This turned out to be what I needed (even though it sucked) in order to make me slow down. God had to take me through a valley of "blah" in order to realize the need to rest.

Rest is not easy for me. It's not natural and it makes me feel lazy. But in that season, I know it's what I needed. I couldn't keep up the hectic pace and continue to be a great mom to our four kids and the one growing inside me. The pregnancy opened my eyes and instead of dreading slowing down, I felt a peace at the thought. I always thought that if I slowed down, I would fall behind. I realized that in order to fulfill my calling, I had to follow God's lead and allow Him to work in every season.

To everything there is a season, a time for every activity under Heaven. Ecclesiastes 3:1

Weaknesses

Most are shocked to hear me say that I've never experienced anxiety. I realize this is a common dilemma for women in our society. I'm not saying it to brag. I'm just announcing it so that God can be glorified in that I believe he gave me a high tolerance for chaos. My friends say this is how I can have so many kids and still be joyful, on top of things and able to handle the crazy. I have to admit that this may be very true but it's not to say I don't have issues of my own to deal with. I've learned about myself that one of my main issues, if you will, is the desire to be fully known.

So instead of saying "We're so busy" when someone asks how you're doing, what if we simply replied with "I'm blessed"? Let's take out the need to be busy and instead focus on spending Sunday evenings sitting on the back porch, sipping sweet tea and planning the week ahead. Let's take Saturday mornings to spring clean or take our kids to the park instead of running from one activity to the next. Let's say no to the illusion of having to pack our schedules. Let's say yes to some margin. I'm right there with ya, girlfriend.

COVID-19

At the time this book releases, I'm not sure what will be going on with this pandemic, the Coronavirus. This year, 2020, this crazy virus spread rampantly throughout the world, starting in Asia, invading Europe and then making its way into the United States. It was swift, very contagious and unlike anything anyone living had ever witnessed before. For the first time anyone I knew could remember, there was a nationwide quarantine. Businesses closed, all restaurants closed their dining rooms, schools closed for weeks and months for some. It was unbelievable. It's still unfathomable to think this virus could turn our thriving economy upside down, disrupt the housing market, cost jobs and threaten so many human lives.

One positive thing that it brought about was the ability for families to come together. It forced everyone to let go of busyness. Most mid-large size companies were forced to send their employees to work at home. Everyone had to stay home, find things to do together, spend quality time together and embrace each other during an uncertain time. We all played games with our kids, read books, did puzzles and treasured the time we had. It caused a shift in mentality, a slowdown. And maybe, just maybe, one day, that's something we will all be thankful for.

I heard this song one day when I was feeling down, as everyone in the nation, maybe even the world was feeling. It inspired me! Just read these lyrics and then listen to the song.

The weapon may be formed, but it won't prosper.
When the darkness falls, it won't prevail.
'Cause the God I serve knows only how to triumph.
My God will never fail.
Oh, my God will never fail.

I'm gonna see a victory.
I'm gonna see a victory.
For the battle belongs to You, Lord.
I'm gonna see a victory.
I'm gonna see a victory.
For the battle belongs to You, Lord.

There's power in the mighty name of Jesus.
Every war He wages He will win.
I'm not backing down from any giant.
'Cause I know how this story ends.
Yes, I know how this story ends.

I'm gonna see a victory.
I'm gonna see a victory.
For the battle belongs to You, Lord.
I'm gonna see a victory.
I'm gonna see a victory.
For the battle belongs to You, Lord.
I'm gonna see a victory.
I'm gonna see a victory.
For the battle belongs to You, Lord.
I'm gonna see a victory.

I'm gonna see a victory.
For the battle belongs to You, Lord.

You take what the enemy meant for evil
And You turn it for good.
You turn it for good.
You take what the enemy meant for evil
And You turn it for good.
You turn it for good.
You take what the enemy meant for evil
And You turn it for good.

I'm gonna see a victory.
I'm gonna see a victory.
For the battle belongs to You, Lord.
I'm gonna see a victory.
I'm gonna see a victory.
For the battle belongs to You, Lord.
Elevation Worship

Are you wearing busyness as a trophy? How can you be more intentional with your time?

_____
_____
_____

CHAPTER 5: COMPARISON

Peace I leave with you; my peace I give you. I do not give as the world gives. Do not let your hearts be troubled and do not be afraid. John 14:27

"STOP EXPECTING TO HAVE A TESTIMONY WITH NO TEST." - PASTOR STEVEN FURTICK

GOAL OF THE CHAPTER: STOPPING THE COMPARISON GAME, FOR YOUR SANITY, MINDSET AND OVERALL WELL-BEING.

Man, oh man, comparison is definitely overrated. If you're like me, or any other woman on the planet, comparison can eat at you if you let it. It can bring you down, damper your mood and affect your days. No one loves competition more than me. Oftentimes, I won't even play a game if I don't think I can win. Competition can be healthy. Comparison is usually distracting and detrimental.

There are two ways to think about comparison: who are you comparing yourself to that is a step above you and who are you allowing to fester your attitude based on how they feel about you. We all compare, we just do. It's a natural human characteristic yet not a fun one. It's how we learn to deal with it that can make all the difference.

Even as I run a flourishing real estate business, I have to stay on top of my thoughts and not let negativity get in my mind. There is always more I could be doing, more I could be achieving, and that woman over there just makes it look so easy! As I stepped into my role as a speaker, it's so easy to look at women who have already made it and think "I'll never be as good as her." or "She must have had it so easy". Lies, all lies, that we tell ourselves. I know that to be true in my own life. From the outside looking in, it looks like my success has come easily, naturally, without any struggle. The outsiders don't see the late nights, countless hours, challenges overcome and everything that comes with building something from the ground up. Take a look at this iceberg illusion - it's one of my favorites.

THE ICEBERG ILLUSION

The point of this illusion is that you don't know what other people go through. You don't know what they have faced in order to get to where they are today. Our paths are so different from anyone else's. We are a combination of all the choices we make every day and of the choices we have made over the course of our lifetime. Chances are people who are successful have faced failure and disappointment. They have sacrificed, developed good habits and learned persistence and hard work. Things don't just happen for most people. You only see the tip of the iceberg when the foundation of it, the majority of it, is buried down below. Ponder that the next time you compare your life with someone who is a step above where you want to be!

Here's the thing, every moment we spend comparing, it's just a waste. It's a waste of time, resources and emotion. And it's not helping us move forward. In fact, it's likely taking us a step back. Pastor Steven Furtick says "What are you going to do with the 750,000,000 breaths God gives you?" He explains that your gifts, abilities, talents and desires are not really yours in the first place. God placed them inside you. You don't get to choose whether or not to use them. It is your obligation to use them.

The Underdog

Attitude of a champion: Work like the underdog.

This is a quote that I read and it jumped out at me. Probably because it's so natural for me to work super hard and never quit. I was raised on a small farm by two self-employed parents. Being a hard worker was instilled in me at an early age. My personality type, being a prior athlete and my chosen career path just exemplifies my work ethic.

I often say that in my job, I know I am not the best. I realize that and I own it. I'm not the smartest, not the most skilled, not a lot of things. But I will outwork anyone. I will communicate better, care more and work harder than any other agent you will find. That's what sets me apart.

Work ethic is what sets apart the mediocre from the excellent. Work ethic is the X factor. My business partner and I have discussed and decided that we will look for two things when interviewing and bringing on new members into our group - do they have the personality for the job and do they have the work ethic? If the answer is no on either, we pass on them. Sometimes, it's hard to determine work ethic right off the bat. Sometimes, it takes time to prove whether a person has it or they don't. But it always comes out in the end. Work ethic shines through.

The thing about being the underdog is that you always have to keep fighting and you never get to stop, slow down or quit. There is no down time, no breaks and no time-outs. Underdogs don't get to bow out for a while at a time. They keep going. Even after they reach success, they keep going. I want to always work like an underdog. No, it's not easy but it keeps me busy, sharp and active. And I know I'll always come on top if my mindset is that of the underdog.

Social Media

I'm going to go out on a limb here and talk about a hot topic. I love social media as much as anyone and I'm super active on it. I enjoy it, I love people and I love communicating. The problem is with the perception, the consumption and the feelings that social media can bring with it.

Why do we have to care so much about what other people say or think? Why does it matter? Why do we feel that we need approval and validation? I don't know the reason. I don't get it and I don't like it. God made us to care but also to be resilient and most importantly, to cast our concerns and our cares upon Him. When our priorities shift, so does our outlook. When our focus shifts, so do our feelings.

I know social media can be a black hole, a place we get stuck in and end up caring way too much about. Social media has so many advantages: friendships, business, promotion, sharing encouragement. All of these are good and useful!

But what happens when we start counting the likes, searching for meaning and motive in comments, and basing our mood on our online presence. That's where the problem occurs and that's where we have to put a stop to it.

I've learned that we cannot base our worth on how others view us, respond to us and react to us. We cannot count likes to determine our value. We cannot spend so much time on it that it encompasses us. We cannot let it define us.

If it's doing that to you, you're not alone. I've been there. Really, I have felt it and it stinks. It hurts and it's crippling. If you are feeling that way, take a few moments here and write down how you are feeling and how you can make it better.

Social media makes me feel:

_____
_____

Here are a few words to choose from if you need some help. Circle the ones that apply to you:

Alive, Inspired, Loved, Meaningful, Happy, Disliked, De-valued, Unmotivated, Unworthy, Mistreated, Less Than, Sad, Mad, Disrespected, Appreciated, Validated.

Now, let's break this down. Did you circle more positive or negative words? If you circled more positive, awesome! You have a healthy relationship with social media. If there are more negative words, let's work on it! Here are a few steps to make you feel better when you're online:

Delete any friends that are constantly negative.

Add friends that are inspiring and post uplifting content.
Post things that make others smile.
Limit your time daily and weekly.
Use it to your advantage but not to your downfall.

Social media was created to be just that, social. It's made to be fun, engaging and ever-changing. Use your light to pour into others. Don't wait for the light, be it. Be it in a dark world that so desperately needs it. Social media can be just one of the platforms you use.

Authentic

I'm going to be real and share a serious and sad reality with you. When you get older, you have a few babies and your body changes, so do other little things. Now, when I sneeze, I better not have to pee at all because my bladder cannot handle the pressure. I know, I know, TMI (Too Much Information). My husband thinks it's gross, but after having kids and an ever-changing body, not much bothers me anymore. Can you agree?

This is something I may not share publicly, but here I am, sharing it with all you readers. It's because I feel connected to you. I wrote this book for you. I wrote it for women who want to feel like someone else gets them, like they are known and that they can be real.

Authenticity is a real thing, a good thing, a motivating thing to others if we use it wisely and well. I love sharing stories with other women that they can relate to! It's important to be real, but not to show all your mess. People crave authenticity, they really do. They crave people with whom they can say "me too". However, they also need someone they can respect. So have fun, share your stories, be real, be open but keep it clean and keep respect for yourself!

Ask these questions before sharing:

Does this enhance my appearance or hurt it?

Does it make me more relatable?
Does it help people see the real me?
Will it make someone laugh?
Will it have a negative impact on my reputation?

I am referring to posting things online, sharing stories in public or with a group of friends. Think before you share, before you air your laundry and definitely before you do something that will stick in others' minds, maybe even forever.

Kind Yet Firm

These two words have become my go-to. They are applicable in most any situation. I am able to use them as I take on challenges, have tough conversations and deal with people. The phrase that I have adopted is this "Be kind yet firm".

These are my two words when dealing with any tough situation. When I need to have a conversation with someone, I try to remember these two words. It's a good reminder to be kind with my words yet firm with their intention and the way they are voiced. I want whoever I am speaking with to understand that I'm serious with what I am saying, yet I want to say the words in a way that represent my faith and myself well.

Sometimes it's tough to have those conversations, whether with an employee or a friend, when we need to have a conversation, these two words will help us have it in a powerful way.

I often use this with my kids as well. They need to hear Mom say things in a kind way that makes them feel safe and loved. But, they need to know that I am serious and mean what I say. That's where the firm part comes in. It's a good way to ensure things will get done, change or be resolved. And if they aren't, at least you can say you have put your best foot forward and made the necessary steps and actions with words you can be proud of at the end of the day.

Kind yet firm is a good approach to letting people know you are serious, you are knowledgeable, you are for real. Kind yet firm sets you apart and it sets you up for success. Kindness makes any situation better and kindness is always a good approach. But kindness needs a sidekick and that's where firmness comes in. Firmness is needed to show that you mean what you say and commands a certain respect. Use this phrase the next time you need to do something, even if you're "doing it afraid" (wink, wink).

The Uncomfortable

When Baker was approaching four-years-old, he fell off the chair and broke his collarbone. He had fallen off the couch and chair dozens of times. He was a constant wrestler with his siblings. He has just always been a rough and tumble little boy! I supposed he just hit it in the right way at the right time. It was a painful break for him and he complained that his "shoulder" hurt. We got x-rays and a sling and then started the long process of wearing it for 4 to 6 weeks. For a three-year-old, that's an eternity! The sling was something new, something unknown and definitely something unwanted. Surprisingly, he liked the sling. He liked the way it made his arm feel better. He wanted it on and recognized the benefit of having his arm lifted. Thankfully, that was helpful!

Sometimes, it's hard for us to remember that what is meant to help us can appear hurtful. It can be cumbersome, uncomfortable or even painful. But, when we are given the right tools and push past the discomfort, sometimes those little tools can make a world of difference! Sometimes, those things can make a huge impact and affect our entire process of our growth!

We must push past discomfort a lot of times in life. We are often pushed out of our comfort zones and are given things that we did not ask for, not even close. But when we do make the choice to push through, make the changes and take the step out, our comfort level shifts and we become much more comfortable with being uncomfortable.

Jealousy

Jealousy is the thief of joy, friendship and harmony. Jealousy ruins friends, relationships and partnerships. Jealousy can sneak in, even if it's given a small space to do so. I've witnessed jealousy doing just that in some of my friendships over the years. It happens so quickly and sometimes, without our consent. It's not always avoidable and it's not always our fault. But it is something to be aware of at all times.

If jealous is creeping into a relationship, keep a close eye on it and smash it if at all possible. Do it quickly and without waiting. If you're the one who is feeling jealousy, don't be afraid to have a difficult conversation and kill it before it kills your relationship.

Jealousy can lead to so much negativity and I've faced my share of it. I've dealt with plenty of mean girls. And here's the truth, there will always be mean girls, no matter how old we are. There are just as many now, in my 30's, as there were when I was in high school. They just look different. And we have more options to avoid them and make better friends than we did in high school. It's important to push away the jealous people looking to see you fail. Trust me there will be plenty. That's one thing that makes it such fun to succeed! If you need this to give you a boost and fuel your drive, use it. Don't let it consume you but let it propel you!

Sing this song with the tune of the George Straight song "Just Give It Away". I wrote my own lyrics. Funny but true. Enjoy!

Just Give It Away
The stress and the anxiety, the all work and the no play.
Just give it away, just give it away.

The wishing and the wanting, the comparing all day.
Just give it away, just give it away.

The bitterness and loneliness, it only hurts you every day.

Oh just give it away, just give it away.

The source of the comparison, they're not worth it anyway.
So just give it away, just give it away,

How does comparison make you feel? How can you say goodbye to it for good?

_____
_____

CHAPTER 6: WAITING

Be strong and courageous. Don't be fearful or discouraged, because the Lord your God is with you wherever you go. Joshua 1:9

"WE MAY IMPRESS PEOPLE WITH OUR STRENGTHS. BUT WE CONNECT WITH THEM THROUGH OUR WEAKNESSES." -PASTOR CRAIG GROESCHEL

GOAL OF THE CHAPTER: MOVING AHEAD IN YOUR CALLING... WITHOUT ALL THE WAITING.

Oh...waiting. Waiting is so overrated. Waiting is the opposite of what God calls us to do when he calls us to move forward in faith. God will always call us to go first. Things will never fall into our laps. Waiting means pursuing, believing, and moving. Here is one phrase my Pastor says and I love it - "The pressure is good for you". We all face pressure: at our jobs, at home, in our own heads. Pressure is real and if you don't have it, you need a little bit of it. Pressure pushes us forward and helps make us better! Waiting requires no pressure, no stretching and no hurting. Waiting is safe and easy. Pursuing with passion is risky.

It's a common human reaction. If you're unsure, just wait. If you're scared, just wait. If you're not ready, just wait. I'm here to challenge that mindset and help you move past the waiting mindset. The best thing I've ever done in my life and my business is to start before I'm ready. I'll say that again in case you breezed over it before. This is powerful: Start before you are ready.

I'm kind of known for doing things afraid and stepping out in faith. Waiting is not necessary in my vocabulary. I believe that waiting for things to be perfect, for everything to line up and waiting for the "right time" well, it's overrated.

Here are the reasons I've found that cause women to wait.

Scarcity- Whether this is a true fear of failure or a scarcity mindset, both are dangerous. Both are crippling. Both are consuming. The easiest way to get out of this mindset is to start shifting your own. What are you afraid of right now? How could you step outside your comfort zone and confront fear head on. The way to quit being afraid is to face fear.

Laziness- Sometimes it's just easier not to do something than to put the work in to get it done. I'm going to go ahead and call this what it is, laziness. Early in 2020, Kobe Bryant, NBA superstar, passed away from an unexpected helicopter crash. I saw this quote that he said earlier in his career:

*"I don't understand lazy people. I don't want to understand them."
-Kobe Bryant*

Take this quote to heart. If you can't relate to it, then learn from it. If you yourself tend to be lazy, make yourself get up and start putting the work in. You'll soon be on the other side of laziness.

Perfection- Many women wait because they are afraid of things not being perfect. Let me give you some truth, things will NEVER be perfect, like ever. Conditions will never be right. You will never know it all. You will never be fully ready. Just start. You'll figure it out along the way. Stop waiting for perfection. It's a myth anyway.

Chocolate Syrup

I walked into the kitchen and my not quite two-year-old was covered in chocolate syrup. The floor was also slathered in it and he was smiling happily with his chocolate-covered mouth. I guess he thought I would think it was as funny and delightful as he did. Instead, I took away his sticky treat, began wiping his hands and mouth and cleaned up the big mess! He instantly threw himself back onto the floor and cried, pounded his feet and turned red. All he knew was that he wanted that yummy treat and Mom took it away! But Mom knew that too much chocolate meant too much sugar which would mean no nap and a sugar crash. It would also mean an even bigger mess to clean up! It was not the best for anyone involved.

I couldn't help but think of this in our relationship with God. He has to take away things from us that we see as good for us, even if it only tastes good in the moment. It's not His best for us. In return, we can protest, cry and withdraw. All we know is that we want to be happy! We want to be satisfied and we want to have fun! How dare God take away the temporary when He knows our future?

When we look at this in relation to the chocolate syrup, it helps us realize that the sticky, sweet, soothing things in this life are not always what are best for us. It's often not what God wants for us long term. God knows our future and ultimately the path we need to take. And sometimes, that means taking away temporary pleasures for eternal results!

Needed But Not Appreciated

Everyone needs me, yet no one appreciates me. I guess this is just part of being a Mom, but it sure isn't the fun part. As Moms, we don't get to sit down after the kids go to bed because we still have to lay out clothes, pack lunches and prepare for the next day. Sometimes, I am envious of my husband as he relaxes easily in his recliner right after putting the kids down. Sometimes, I wish I could do that but it's not in the cards in this season. I have to get my work done that has been pushed to the back burner during the day and make sure everyone is ready to go for the next day! Rest can come later, when I finally make myself stop and sit down about an hour later.

As a wife and a mom of many, gosh, it's pretty common to feel like you're needed everywhere you turn. It's also pretty normal to never get a thank you or a word of encouragement for your hard work and taking care of everyone and fulfilling all their needs. Being a mom is a very "thankless" and "selfless" job. It's one that requires you to sense your kids' needs at every hour, constantly be on call and play the part of: nurse, chef, chauffeur and everything in between. We kiss boo-boos and wipe tears, run schedules and offer encouragement and love. It's all consuming and honestly, nothing can prepare you for it.

Most days, I can roll without needing a thank you but other days are harder. What gets me through is the hug and kiss at night, right before bedtime with sweet prayers together and story time. At that time, I know that I am loved, needed, wanted. I then go take a shower and soak in a few minutes of alone time before going to spend the rest of the evening with my husband. It's a good life, even though sometimes it's a crazy life.

Outside Our Comfort Zones

As my friend Lysa Terkurst says (I call Lysa my friend even though we have never met), "Outside our comfort zone is where we experience the true awesomeness of God". In her book "What Happens When Women Say Yes to God", I was moved, awed and humbled. I felt the call to live a life pleasing to God and way outside my comfort zone. I have always been pretty good about not sticking inside a comfort zone. I'm not afraid of risks, which is why I have been able to accomplish some pretty crazy things. But, man, comfort zones are comfy. And once we get in them, we just want to stay in them. They are like a warm blanket, so cozy and fuzzy, that we just want to stay. But, comfort zones were never meant to be lived in. Women who move outside of them confidently, can live a life like few others get to experience. Here are some things you can expect when you choose to live outside your comfort zone:

- *Mountaintop Moments*
- *Valleys that will teach you more than mountaintops ever could*
- *Trials and testing*
- *Favor of God*
- *A wild ride*

Even the scary moments, the hard times, the times God uses to teach us, they are worth it. For we know that he will work all things to the good of those who love him. God loves to take ordinary people who will step outside their comfort zones and do extraordinary things through them. He proves that all throughout the Bible. The question is, will that be you?

Waiting for More

You know what's totally overrated, feeling like we can and should do it all. Like what the heck? When did we feel like we needed to be Super Woman all the time? It took me a while to feel like I deserved to give some things away. Like, I deserved to delegate some things in my life in order to free up more time. I made a list of all the things I did every week and then I crossed off the things that were time consuming, unnecessary, or didn't bring me joy. The unnecessary things were crossed off for good. The time consuming things that only I could do were moved up into a priority category. The time consuming things that didn't bring me joy and could be delegated were put on a separate list and here is the kicker, I hired someone else to do those things for me! Here is a snapshot of my list of things I am responsible for each week:

- Laundry
- Kids' morning drop-off
- Kids' afternoon pick-up
- Dishes
- Cooking
- Grocery pick-up
- House deep cleaning

- Coaching clients
- Running the business
- Working with my clients
- Writing
- Speaking
- Working out
- Packing kids lunches
- Helping kids with homework
- Kids activities
- Processing paperwork for business
- Business bookkeeping.

Now take a look at the list once I went through it and categorized it:

Family - Non-Negotiables - ME (with help of husband)
Church
Kids' morning drop-off
Kids' afternoon pick-up
Packing kids lunches
Helping kids with homework
Kids' activities
Supper/Bedtime/Bath

Household - Negotiable
Laundry - HIRE
Dishes - ME
Cooking - ME
Grocery pick-up - HIRE
House deep cleaning - HIRE
Household bills - ME (and husband)

Business - Negotiable
Coaching clients - ME
Running the business - ME (and my partner)
Working with my clients - ME
Writing - ME

ASHLEY SCHUBERT

Speaking - ME
Working out - ME
Processing paperwork for business - HIRE
Business bookkeeping - HIRE

When I broke these things down and saw how much I actually do each week, it made me feel better about giving some things away. Now, I can get so much accomplished and I don't have to do "all the things". All the things are getting done, which is an amazing feeling, but I'm not physically doing it all. I get asked a lot about how I do it all and make it look so easy. It's because I'm intentional, I have a plan, I get help from those I reach out to and hire to do the tasks necessary for me to function at my best. It feels so good to give those things away. It was hard at first, because I want to feel like I can do it all. But who am I trying to impress? The answer for me was myself, my husband, and everyone who viewed me as Super Woman. But here's the thing, Super Woman doesn't exist. So be your own kind of Super Woman and get yourself some help. Prioritize your schedule and your needs, find the areas where you need help and MAKE IT HAPPEN.

So write out your week and your responsibilities right now:

_____
_____
_____
_____
_____
_____

Now, what can you delegate that would help you tremendously:

_____
_____
_____
_____
_____

This will be awkward at first and you will feel the need to pick some things back up. You may need to look over your budget and see what you're willing to spend in order to make some of these things happen. You'll then need to determine if it's worth it to you. Here's what you need to remember - ONLY DO WHAT ONLY YOU CAN DO. If you want to be successful, get rid of stress and be an achiever, you must prioritize what only you can do and be thankful to delegate the rest.

Always There

Beauty is always there. It's just sometimes hidden.

Love is always there. It's just sometimes overshadowed.

Positivity is always there. Negativity just sometimes overwhelms it.

Hope is always there. Defeat just sometimes seems easier.

Joy is always there. The choice to choose joy is just sometimes harder.

Ashley Schubert, 2020

What are you waiting for? Make a plan NOW.

_____
_____
_____
_____

CHAPTER 7: OTHERS OPINIONS

On the day I called, You answered me; You made me bold with strength in my soul. Psalm 138:3

"BEING CONSUMED BY WHAT PEOPLE THINK OF YOU IS THE FASTEST WAY TO FORGET WHAT GOD THINKS OF YOU." -PASTOR CRAIG GROESCHEL

GOAL OF THE CHAPTER: GETTING OVER WHAT OTHERS THINK AND REALIZING IT WAS NEVER ABOUT THEM ANYWAY.

Opinions are so overrated. I once read that "Your life isn't your own if you are constantly worried about others' opinions". There is a lot of truth in that statement.

This is a chapter that is all too familiar to me. It's one that I struggle with because, no matter how hard I try, others' opinions matter to me. I care what others think and I want to please. I've definitely gotten better about not letting it consume me but it's a struggle and I'm not afraid to admit it. Instead of dwelling on it, I've chosen to use it to raise me up, make me better and ultimately, give glory to God.

God bless us for thinking we can love others without His help and without His divine and utter grace. We need Him to help us love others, those that He created, those that He has called us to love. When I don't feel that love in my heart, I have to turn and question my own motives and look inside my own heart. Is there something dark living inside there, maybe hidden so well that only I know it's back there? If my spiritual life is in a funk, it's going to bleed into my relationships, my attitude and how I feel about others.

"We love others best when we love God most." - Kyle Idleman

This is one of the hardest things I've dealt with in my current season and to be honest, for my whole life. It's so easy to fall back into old patterns and allow opinions to consume your thought patterns. I don't want to be controlled by what others believe to be true about me and I'm over it. My attitude, my joy and my self-esteem should not be dictated by what someone else thinks or says about me. Even though I know this to be true, it doesn't make it any easier to live out each day.

I can think of individuals right now that don't like me, or I don't think they like me, or they don't act like they like me. They never seem happy to see me succeed and would likely be much happier to just see me fail. But if I give into those negative thoughts and allow them to permeate my mood, my heart and my soul, it does nothing but affect me negatively. It creates bitterness in me and distracts me from what matters. When that happens, it affects and limits my true calling. And that's truly a shame.

"Don't wait for other people to be loving, giving, compassionate, grateful, forgiving, generous, or friendly...lead the way!"

Tackling Fuel

Have you ever watched the movie The Water Boy? It's a movie starring Adam Sandler, who plays a college football player who must learn to live and thrive in a new world in which he doesn't fit in. It's a comedy and he often gets teased because he is "different". However, he learns to channel that negativity and those harsh words spoken against him and his coach teaches him to think of it as his "tackling fuel". I can still hear him saying this phrase in my mind. If you have seen the movie, I'm sure you can too! It's hilarious to make this comparison because the movie is really meant to be a funny tale that is in no way serious. But I cannot help but compare this to the way we must treat those in our life who speak negatively against us. We can either choose to give in to those thoughts and let them win. Or, we can use what others meant to destroy us and channel it into our "tackling fuel". That fuel can give us the drive to push forward, keep working hard, believing in ourselves and going toward the goal God set before us.

For me, I've noticed that most of the people who will speak negatively over my life don't do it by sending me a mean text or publicly blasting me. They may not even do it by giving me the stink eye or walking by without saying hello (even though those things do happen). What is most common is that those who wish negativity toward us just cast doubt in our mind, make us doubt ourselves and doubt our dream. I've certainly questioned my leadership abilities, my dreams, my overall personality and heart and more! It's so sad to say, but negative people have made me question whether or not I should pursue my God given abilities and passions. Maybe you can relate. It's sad yet true to admit it and admitting it feels good.

Instead of giving in to these thoughts, which are in no way true or productive, I choose regularly to use them as "tackling fuel". I use them to push me forward, inspire me, and say "get behind me, Satan", since he is actually the deceiver and destroyer of all things in which God designed. I can use negative energy of others, jealousy, bad wishes and stink eyes and I can push forward toward my true calling. The one I know that lives inside me, the one that you know lives inside you. The choice is yours: crouch down and be destroyed or use it as your tackling fuel to move forward? Choose wisely.

The Trouble With The Three

As much as God has taught me about my parenting style during the writing of this book, He has taught me just as much about my inner self and why I am the way I am. I have wrestled with some thoughts and feelings that I've never had to consider before. I've had to realize that I am not what I achieve. I am who God says I am. Being a 3 on the Enneagram means that I am super achievement driven, very performance based, and my worth comes from feeling like I am seen as successful. This can be great when it comes to achievement, because I can deliver over and over again. Mostly because I do whatever it takes to win and I don't stop until I get there. Looking back, I believe this stems from my childhood. My Mom was proud of me when I achieved on the basketball court, when I scored enough points, when I played well! When I didn't, I didn't receive any praise and it hurt. I got used to performing in order to feel love. It's weird thinking back on that and reliving those feelings but it's helped me understand where I am now and why. It's made me realize that I want to show my kids love and acceptance no matter what, not just on their performance. I pray I am able to do that and show that!

It is a decision daily for me to find my value, my worth, in who God says I am, in being His child, in being loved by Him.

I hardly ever cry. I'm not an emotional person by any means. Being an athlete and a first born meant I always had to be strong. I was always the leader and leaders have to lead with strength. Although, I've learned that the best leaders lead through the pain, through the raw and through the mess. Pastor Craig Groeschel says "People would rather follow a leader who is always real than one who is always right".

My husband and I had a discussion recently and I actually cried. He is the only person who ever gets to see that side of me. It was regarding our upcoming baby being born and whether I planned to take some time off. You see, I've had four babies, and never taken maternity leave, never taken a break. I've always been so consumed with working, achieving and being perceived as "being able to do it all". It's subconscious but I realize that's the "why" behind it. I told him that this time I planned to take a month off from work. I don't know what I expected but I didn't expect his response "Why would you do that?" I was floored. "Because, I want to", I replied. "Because, I can", "Because I've worked hard for 8 years in this business so that I can take some time off and still be okay". I burst into tears (so unlike me) and he instantly felt bad. After some time of discussion, I was able to voice my true feelings. I had never taken time off because I wanted HIM to be proud of me. I wanted him to see that I could do it all and never miss a beat. I wanted him to brag on me, hold me in high regard and never doubt my strength. The problem was that he never expected any of that from me. He didn't expect me to have it all together, didn't expect me to do it all and certainly didn't need me to perform in order to be proud of me. WOW! He said "Babe, you don't have to work another day in your life and I would still be proud of you. You don't have anything to prove to me". A weight was lifted off my chest. I suddenly knew that it was okay to take a break, okay to plan for some time off, okay to not have to justify my decision. This conversation allowed me to know that my husband was rooting for me, no matter what. I have a hard time being vulnerable because I worry about how I will be perceived. But, vulnerability allows an open door for conversation, communication and walls to come down.

Taking a break is going to be hard for me. Rest is hard for me. But I'm planning for it, I'm believing for it and I'm praying God grants me the peace to be able to fully rest in His abundance. I'm learning more and growing each day. His grace is truly sufficient.

Pushing Through The Blah

Do you ever have days that are just "blah"? Not good, not bad, just kind of in the middle. Sometimes, this may go in seasons and feel like it lasts longer than just a day or two. Do you ever have times when you feel like Satan knows right where to hit you? For me, Satan knows to make me question my leadership abilities and whether or not I have any friends who care about me. He knows the areas that make me question myself and penetrating my thoughts with these things gets me down and discouraged. The enemy knows where to hit us and unfortunately, he is good at it. It's in these seasons and days that we must push past that the "blah" and move forward in God's truth.

Fill your mind with positive thoughts through things that will make you feel happy, inspired and hopeful. It's a great idea to listen to music and podcasts that uplift you. It's a good idea to go for a walk outside and enjoy some sunshine. It's a good idea to plan for something ahead that you can be excited about. It's amazing to count your blessings and realize what you already have to be happy about!

These times are not easy, they are trying, and they are in no way fun. But they also teach us to rely on God heavily, trust in Him fully and look forward to better days ahead!

What is God teaching you right now that is proving to be difficult?

_____
_____

What are some ways you can fill yourself with positivity?

_____
_____

Winners focus on Winning

Did you watch the Summer Olympics in 2016? Chances are you did and hopefully you got to watch Michael Phelps win historic gold medals in swimming, over and over again! It was truly magical to watch and so memorable to behold. In one race, he was facing a South African swimmer who seemed to be fully determined to psych Michael out. Instead of focusing on his own warm up routine, this guy was very visibly trying to get into Michael's head by shadow boxing in the corner and just doing strange things to make his appearance known. If you have never seen this, look it up on YouTube and watch the video. It's one of the greatest moments in Olympic history in my opinion. You see, this guy was so focused on distracting Michael and making him lose the race that he totally forfeited his opportunity to focus on his own race ahead. When it came time for the race, Michael Phelps showed his true colors, kept his head forward and won the race easily. The opponent who was so focused on distracting him didn't even place. That guy was a great swimmer and had won his fair share of awards. If he had just focused on his own talents, his outcome could have been very different. Instead, he kept his head to the side, watched his opponent, and focused only on seeing him be defeated. And this is where this quote comes into play: "Winners focus on winning. Losers focus on winners."

You will notice that some people are so much more focused on seeing others fail, that they don't spend any time working on their own success. Don't fall into this trap of comparison, doubt and blindness. When you are blind to your own potential, you focus solely on others successes and that leads straight to bitterness.

Instead of watching others highlight reels, focus on your own mission. Focus on what is placed before you. Worry about your own vision and move forward knowing that winners focus on winning.

Fan the Flame

It's Satan's overall goal to knock us down, make us feel unworthy and diminish our God given gifts. He does this in any way he can, including working through other people. He wants us to feel defeated. But, in God, we always have the ultimate victory! I wrote this during a difficult time when I was feeling crushed and God reminded me to fan the flame he placed inside of me.

Fan the Flame

Sometimes, I get defeated. People will let you down. Others will root for you to fail. Some still, will doubt you.

Sometimes, I question my own gifts, abilities and calling. It's hard to stay on fire and passionate all the time, especially when you question yourself.

Sometimes, I feel confused and conflicted and I don't know if I'm doing enough, being enough...I'm never enough for everyone.

And then I read this...

For this reason I remind you to fan into flame the gift of God, which is in you through the laying on of my hands. 2 Timothy 1:6

So, my flame I'll keep on fanning, until God extinguishes my fire.

I may get knocked down but I'm not destroyed. In Him, I am enough.

Fan the flame.

Ashley Schubert, 2020

What can you let go of? Anger, bitterness, hurt, betrayal? How can this help you move forward and "fan the flame"?

_____
_____
_____

CHAPTER 8: PERFECTION

And hope does not put us to shame, because God's love has been poured into our hearts through the Holy Spirit who has been given to us. Romans 5:5

"PEOPLE WOULD RATHER FOLLOW A LEADER WHO IS ALWAYS REAL THAN ONE WHO IS ALWAYS RIGHT." -PASTOR CRAIG GROESCHEL

GOAL OF THE CHAPTER: DETERMINING THAT PERFECTION WAS AND ALWAYS WILL BE OVERRATED.

If there is one thing I know for sure it's this, perfection is overrated. Yet, we are obsessed with this idea of perfection being attainable. Y'all, it's a myth, a hoax and I am here to uncover it and expose it for what it is. Most women who seem to have it "figured out" have just learned how to be comfortable in their own skin and embrace who they are. They have learned to not care what others think and be boldly who God called them to be.

When I was playing basketball in high school, bruises on my legs were super common. I was a pretty scrappy player. So, it was not uncommon for my legs to be covered in bruises each week from diving and rolling around on the gym floor, fighting for the ball. I wore those bruises like a trophy because it meant I had played. I had worked hard. I had fought and I had earned those blue and black things. I was never embarrassed of them and in fact, I would flaunt them. They were a badge of courage and strength.

During this fifth pregnancy, my varicose veins in my legs have gotten bad, y'all. Like, they are big and ugly and spreading. They aren't super painful, unless I've been on my feet all day, which sometimes happens. I was able to wear pants for the whole first part of pregnancy, thanks to winter weather and cool Oklahoma winds. And then spring hit and it was time to break out the shorts. I had to make the choice to continue hiding my legs and be hot or to be comfortable and flaunt the veins, big and ugly as they were. I remembered my days of playing basketball and showing off my legs. I had worked for them, earned them and pregnancy was just as honorable as playing a basketball game. The veins would be my badge of courage, I decided. Hopefully, they would go away after pregnancy (I prayed!). But, even if not, I decided that God allowed me to carry babies, birth babies and raise healthy babies and He wouldn't want me to be ashamed of the proof of this. Hiding them, being embarrassed by them and shrinking back would just be denying God of the proof of His goodness. So, if you see me and my veiny black and blue legs, just know that they are my trophies.

Mastering the Messy Bun

This cover was chosen because it symbolizes the lack of perfectionism. You see, it's me...with my signature messy bun. Let me explain. One reason I am able to get ready quickly, take care of a bunch of kids and get so much accomplished each day is because I don't sweat the small stuff. I almost always have on make-up yet hardly ever a complete made-up face. I try to dress nice and stay stylish yet it will never be my top priority. And I don't have my hair down and done very often. That's because I have mastered and own the messy bun. The messy bun, to me, symbolizes the fact that I have accepted what's most important to me right now in life; it's my kids, my home, my business, everything else that needs most of my attention. My hair is certainly not one of them at this point. That's why most often I pull my hair up into a bun, have a two minute fix with hair spray and call it good! The messy bun is easy, effective and it always works.

The messy bun is just a symbol. It's a way to say that your hair doesn't always have to be perfect, your make-up doesn't always have to be done perfectly, your clothes don't always have to be on point and in style. Your kids don't always have to behave perfectly, your floors don't always have to be shiny and you don't always have to have a successful month at work. But, you do have to find what works for you; to feel good in what you wear, with how you look, with how you want to live and how you want to work. It's important to be confident, be polished and be prepared to look and feel your best. Seasons change and maybe in 10 years, when my kids can all dress themselves and fix their own snack, I'll be able to blow dry and curl my hair every day but maybe not. My priority is not my hair. It's getting things done. My hair takes second place (or 11th, outside my top 10). I choose to compromise on my hair so that I can focus on what's important: my kids, my home, my business. It's as simple as that. Perfect hair is overrated.

What are you spending a lot of your time on that is overrated and could be ruled out for now?

1.
2.
3.

Kid's Schedules

I've said it before and I'll say it again. You control your kid's schedule. You sign them up for the activities. You make the choice what they do and what you choose for your family to do. If you want to be successful, remember this "you cannot let your kid's schedules dictate your success". They cannot control you. Maybe that means not playing in a soccer league at age 10 that takes you away from church every weekend and family time every evening. Maybe that means sitting out of gymnastics and instead sitting around the table as a family each evening. Maybe that means finding a sport or an activity that works better for your kids and your lifestyle.

I have talked to too many moms who are totally overwhelmed and over committed because of the activities their kids keep them in non-stop. They are held captive by evening practices and weekend trips. They are broke because of uniforms and league fees. Their families are falling apart because they don't value what matters most. Their businesses are non-existent because they let other things take priority.

Moms, we must show our kids what's most important in life. We must model for them our priorities. We must make church, family time and our goals apparent and noticeable for our kids. That's our job and our responsibility. If we let our schedules control us, we show them that they should do the same thing.

What's running your life right now that you wish you could take control of? Make a plan to do that now.

1.
2.
3.
4.
5.

The Workaholic
I'll be the first to tell you that I enjoy working. I can get consumed and obsessed. Work is a top priority to me. I have seen many friends who work too much and get burned out. Here is what it looks like: getting to work early and staying late consistently, skipping family meals, working late into the night, feeling run down without good sleep, making your kids watch their phones so you can work on your computer and not miss a day. That's working but that's not living.

If that's you, it's okay. It can be fixed. Just get some general guidelines in place. Like this:

> 1. I will leave the office at this time each day.

2. I will have dinner with my family every night.
3. I will make exercise a priority for my body.
4. I will get good sleep each night.
5. I will have date nights without talking about work.
6. I will take my kids to do fun things, to enjoy nature, to be active, on my days off.
7. I will do things that make me happy.
8. I will grow spiritually.

Being a workaholic is not worth it if it affects your body, your family and your overall future. Getting ahead isn't always best. Getting ahead is just a way of life, a choice to make each day. Whether it's worth it or not is completely up to you. Be healthy, be happy and be whole.

Our Plans

If there is anything I have learned in my years of being a Christian it's this: God has bigger plans for us than we could ever have for ourselves. His plans most certainly won't look like ours and I'm sure He laughs when we try to plan out our next decade. Now, I am a huge believer in goal setting and making plans for the future and I will tell you to do so until the cows come home. But that doesn't mean that we are in control. God has bigger plans for us than we could ever imagine and even though we may not know the outcome years in advance, the joy should be found in the journey.

When I was a teenager, I thought I might want to be many things: a news reporter, lawyer, and for a brief time even a whale trainer at SeaWorld (blame it on the Shamu show when I was 13). My dreams of being a whale trainer were crushed when I realized I wasn't a great swimmer. I couldn't go underwater without holding my nose, I couldn't dive and honestly, I didn't like big fish. So, I gave up on that momentary plan of action. I started thinking more reasonably. What would make me happy? What would I be good at doing? I never in a million years thought I would become a real estate agent and open my own brokerage. Like ever! But, here I am, living my dream, just not the one I had in my head. One thing is for sure, God had to take me down some crazy roads, through some disappointments and over some mountains in the process, but here I am, right where I'm supposed to be.

Write down 5 goals/plans for yourself for the next 5 years. Won't it be fun to see how those work out for you!

1. _____
2. _____
3. _____
4. _____
5. _____

Family Planning

I came from a family of two kids. My husband only had one sibling as well. We were both from these small families with parents who were perfectly content with two. And then there we were, young and in love, and we decided we wanted to start the big family. He always said we had to have an even number. "Somebody is always left out if there is an odd number" he said. So we said "let's have 4". Within 6 years, we had 4 children. Crazy, I know. But, remember, crazy is what I do. After the fourth was born, I never felt a sense of completeness. I felt like God was saying "one more". That wasn't our plan. That wasn't on the 10 year dream board. Five kids was never something we planned for but with the stirring in my heart, I couldn't let it go. I was also convinced it would be a girl this time. I wrote this entry in my diary many months before we decided to go for baby #5 and I've never shared it with anyone before.

For the first time ever, I am unsure of this major decision. Are we done having children or should we have one more? Before we had our fourth, I felt God speak to me directly about "our last one" and I knew the fourth didn't feel like the last. The stirring won't go away and our amazing baby boy just turned one. I just released my first book and am busy and our days are full. Should I just push aside this stirring? We have every reason to say "no, we are done". Kids are expensive, a lot of work, time consuming and we are so busy with our jobs. How can we raise another? But, when we say "how", God says "I'll make a way." May God bless us and help us as we feel His peace and guidance in this journey. TBD - 5-2-19

I was so sure when we found out we were pregnant again in October, that this time it would be a girl. But God had other plans. This is a little poem I wrote on the day the ultrasound revealed we were having yet another boy to add to our family.

Another Boy

The Lord must think I have nerves of steel.

He must know I can handle mud, rocks and frogs really well.

A Momma's heart with a love that only being a mother of little boys can be filled.

It's dinosaurs, campfires, sticks and trucks on wheels.

He must believe I am a boy Mom to the core.

A boy Mom I will be with a houseful galore!

Ashley Schubert, 2019

I know this to be true: God's plans are bigger than mine, better than mine and will reach farther than mine ever could. I have chosen to be thankful for the unknown, thankful for the side roads and the detours, even though sometimes they are not fun and not always a joy ride. The journey can be crazy but the destination is always glorious.

Living in the Moments

"Life is not measured by the number of breaths that we take. But by the *moments that take our breath away."*

Here is something to contemplate. How many moments can you think of that literally took your breath away? Write down 5 right now.

1._____
2._____
3._____
4._____
5._____

To be fair, I did the same exercise with you. Here is what I came up with:

> 1. *Walking down the aisle towards my husband on our wedding day.*
> 2. *Every time I delivered one of my babies and saw them for the first time.*
> 3. *Seeing the Eiffel Tower in Paris in person.*
> 4. *Winning homecoming queen my sophomore year of college.*
> 5. *Watching my kids play in the backyard while overlooking our property and counting my blessings.*

Here is the point I'm trying to make. We need to do more things that are breath taking. We need to step out of our comfort zones more and step out in faith. The big moments in life are big for a reason, they are supposed to be! Big moments are meant to feel exhilarating. But all big moments are preceded with risk, trials, saying "yes", some pain and maybe even some doubt. They are always worth it when you get to the other side. Other things have been big moments to me, like winning real estate awards that I worked so tirelessly to earn, like being inducted into the $100,000 Club in my second year of becoming a new realtor. I worked so dad-gum hard for that award. I wanted it so bad. I put that number in front of me every single day. And then I achieved it and it was worth it! It sounds a little selfish for an award to be a big deal, but when you literally put your blood, sweat and tears into something, it tastes so sweet when you finally achieve it. The risk is almost certainly worth the risk, when the reward is so worthy and honestly, the more unattainable the better. I also like the unattainable because it means that God has to intervene in order for the goal to be reached. If He doesn't, there is no way it will be. You give it all you've got, then God. That's the best part. So don't be afraid of stepping out and going for something great. Those moments that will take your breath away are just around the corner!

What perfect plans can you push aside? Trust God today knowing that His ways are best.

_____
_____
_____

"GOD DOESN'T JUST USE THE DESTINATION, BUT THE JOURNEY TO TRAIN YOU HOW TO HEAR HIS VOICE." -PASTOR TD JAKES

AFTERWORD

WAYS TO WIN:

My desire is that these ways to win in each area will inspire you to create the life you want through intentionality and taking the right steps each day. These ways may not all be best for you but maybe some will. You can always add your own in, take some of mine away and make more plans. Most importantly, I hope you make the most of each day you are given!

<u>5 Ways to Win At Home</u>

1. Change out your decor seasonally and move around furniture to create a fresh look.
2. Keep plenty of books handy and visible.
3. Make your bed every single morning.
4. Hire out a responsibility that frees up your time and brings you joy to give away!
5. Plan your week before it begins.

<u>5 Ways to Win With Your Kids at Bedtime:</u>

1. Use the last hour of your day to be fully engaged with your kids - phones down, full attention on them.
2. If they are little, get on the floor and play with them.

3. Listen to them for 5 minutes at night. Let them talk about their day, their friends, whatever they want.
4. Say prayers with them every single night.
5. Stay with a routine as much as possible. Kids crave structure.

5 Ways to Win With Your Family:

1. Eat supper around the table together every night if possible or as much as you possibly can! 2. Go for a walk together in the evenings.
3. Plan a family getaway several times a year, even if it's to a cabin close by where you can enjoy an adventure together.
4. Give hugs constantly and consistently.
5. Say "I Love You" every single day.

5 Ways to Win In Your Marriage:

1. Use positive affirmations.
2. Plan a date night once per month, even if that means arranging a sitter. It's worth it!
3. Kiss and hug goodbye morning and evening. 4. Give a surprise gift from time to time.
5. Use evenings as your time to connect and communicate.

5 Ways to Win In Your Business:

1. Be obsessed or be average.
2. Be better than the average and you will be perceived as great.
3. Work harder than anyone else is willing to. 4. Don't be afraid to take risks and start before you're ready.
5. Be exceptional and be known for what you do.

5 Ways to Win With Your Health:

1. Get physical activity every single day.
2. Eat until you're full and then stop eaing.
3. Move as much as possible.
4. Make your health a priority – doctor's appointments, chiropractor, exercise.
5. Buy a giant water bottle and make it a goal to drink it all every day.

<u>5 Ways to Win in Faith:</u>

1. Start your first 5 minutes each day with God.
2. Make church a non-negotiable priority.
3. Journal about your feelings and what God is teaching you.
4. Listen to Christian music in your car and podcasts that encourage you!
5. Always have a thankful heart.

<u>5 Ways to Win With Your Wardrobe:</u>

1. Clean out your closet once per quarter and get rid of anything you haven't worn all season.
2. Only buy things you absolutely love.
3. Have several signature pieces that you feel beautiful and confident in.
4. Keep at least 5 pairs of classy and simple pieces of jewelry that you love.
5. Know what colors work for you!

<u>5 Ways to Win In Your Kitchen:</u>

1. Go through all your cabinets and get rid of items you don't use.
2. The kitchen is the heart of your home - make sure it gives you a feeling of happiness when you're in it.
3. Light a candle each evening before supper and leave it burning

until bedtime.
4. Plan your meals each week before the week begins.
5. Empty your sink and load your dishwasher every night.

ACKNOWLEDGEMENT

A TRIBUTE TO MY FAMILY:

Bronson - Thank you for giving me the grace and love that it takes to write a book, run a business and raise our babies. One thing is for sure, I could never be on this crazy journey without you. I love this life we have made. God has blessed us so much and I am just happy to be here by your side. Thanks for never telling me I'm crazy and for always believing in my dreams, as I'll always believe in yours.

Brylee - My one and only girl. I love to watch you grow and excel. You are the best sister, daughter, student and so much more! You are an absolute leader. I look forward to our many days together. We have so many great days ahead and our bond will never be broken!

Bowen - My heart, my handful. You will always be both of these things. I love your energy, your kindness, your spirit and your adventurous ways! You just turned 6, but to me, you will always be my little baby boy. I love you forever!

Baker - Thank you for giving me the inspiration to write this book. Thank you for showing me what it means to not be normal and to own it. Thank you for breaking me out of my comfort zone and stretching me to be the mom you need. Thank you for all the days we have together, even though some are challenging. You are special, you are unique and you are a champion. Now, go and soar!

I'll be your biggest fan.

Benaiah - You are and always will be my angel. Your sweet spirit, happy personality and loving nature shines through. You are my sweetheart and you make me happy every single day. Your smile and your eyes are precious and joy radiates through you. Never change, baby boy.

Barlow - At the time I write this, you are still in my belly. You are kicking and happy and strong. Your due date is still about 12 weeks away. So, we will meet you soon! We cannot wait to add you to this crazy clan we call our family. You are already so loved!